CARING FOR THE PLANET
TROPICAL RAINFORESTS

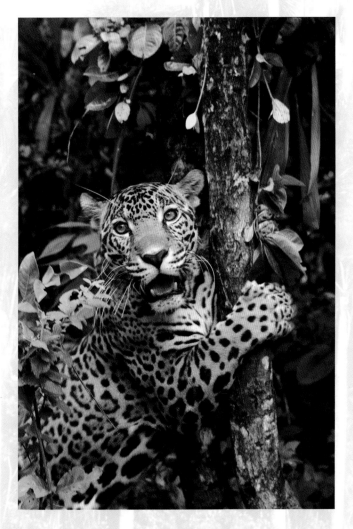

Neil Champion

W
FRANKLIN WATTS
LONDON•SYDNEY

C An Appleseed Editions book

First published in 2006 by Franklin Watts
Reprinted 2007

Franklin Watts
338 Euston Road, London NW1 3BH

Franklin Watts Australia
Level 17/207 Kent St, Sydney, NSW 2000

© 2006 Appleseed Editions

Created by Appleseed Editions Ltd, Well House,
Friars Hill, Guestling, East Sussex, TN35 4ET

Design and production by Helen James

ISBN-10: 0 7496 5994 7
ISBN-13: 978 0 7496 5994 3
Dewey Classification: 333.75

A CIP catalogue for this book is available from the British Library.
Photographs by Getty Images (Jose Azel / Aurora, Dr R Howard Berg, James
P. Blair / National Geographic, Tim Chapman, China Photos, Nicole Duplaix /
National Geographic, Victor Englebert / Time Life Pictures, Peter Essick / Aurora,
Tim Graham, Sarah Leen / National Geographic, Romilly Lockyer, MAYELA
LOPEZ / AFP, H. John Maier Jr. / Image Works / Time Life Pictures, Michael
Melford / National Geographic, Michael Nichols / National Geographic, Michael
K. Nichols / National Geographic, JOEL NITO / AFP, ISSOUF SANOGO / AFP, Joel
Sartore / National Geographic, Maria Stenzel / National Geographic, Roy Toft /
National Geographic, Carl D. Walsh / Aurora, Steve Winter / National Geographic,
Paul A. Zahl / National Geographic)

Franklin Watts is a division of Hachette Children's Books

Contents

Earth is an amazing place. It is complex, beautiful and awe-inspiring. There has been life on it for some three and a half billion years. In all that time, it has grown more complex as life-forms **evolved**. Today, there are more species of plants and animals – about ten million according to one scientific estimate – and more **habitats** in which they live than at any point in Earth's long history. This is our inheritance. It is this that we are changing at a faster rate than ever before. Our ability to alter the environment to suit our own purposes has never been greater. This allows many of us to live longer, more active lives. These are positive things. However, there are sides to our development and expansion that are not so positive for the planet.

The rainforest biome

Environmental scientists divide up the world into large natural zones called biomes. These biomes include rainforests, deserts, **temperate** woodlands, **tundra**, grasslands or prairies, oceans, and rivers and wetlands. Each biome has a certain type of climate and is characterized by its plant and animal life, which is adapted to live in the conditions it offers.

This book looks at life in the rainforest biome and the threats rainforests face today. It also looks at some solutions to these threats that may protect what is left of the natural world.

What is a rainforest?

Rainforests, as their name suggests, are forests that grow in parts of the world that receive a lot of rainfall. This refers to places in which rainfall occurs consistently throughout the year, rather than regions that see heavy rain for just part of the year. The term usually refers to tropical rainforests, which are found near the equator. But there is also another type of rainforest – temperate rainforest – found on North America's north-west coast, on the South Island of New Zealand and in southern Chile.

Tropical rainforests

Tropical rainforests grow in Central and South America, Africa, Asia and Australia in a belt that follows the equator across these continents. Although they grow in regions widely spread out across the globe, all tropical rainforests show very similar characteristics. They are all ancient and complex environments, needing a climate that provides constant daily rain – with a total of at least 150 centimetres a year – and a uniform temperature of about 28°C. There are no real seasons in rainforests. The weather feels the same – warm and humid – all year round. Rainforests all share another characteristic as well: all are under threat from human activity and are being cut down at an alarming rate around the world.

Constant growth

All tropical rainforests show a great diversity of life. Between 50 and 200 different types of trees may be found in just one hectare of rainforest. That is 20 times the species found in the most diverse temperate forest. Rainforest trees are mainly evergreen and have broad leaves, many with 'drip tips' for shedding water. The trees lose old leaves but grow new ones at the same time, so they are never leafless. The forests are crowded, and trees grow to enormous heights – often 60–90 metres – in their struggle to catch the light. Their roots are very distinctive, having evolved to hold up the tall trees in soil that is often shallow and of poor quality. The results are huge buttress roots that prop the tree up from its base and amazing-looking stilt roots that stick out from the side of the tree into the ground. The forests also support huge climbing plants, including tough, woody vines called lianas, which can be 200 metres long.

Persistent rain and abundant sunlight promote constant growth in tropical rainforests. Unlike forests further from the equator, the growing season never stops here. Consider winter in America or Europe: leaves fall off most trees, daylight lessens, and the natural world goes into hibernation. Nothing like this happens in a tropical rainforest.

Green forest

The lush green of the rainforest around Lake Sandoval in southern Peru, South America. Fed by the Madre de Dios River, this region sits within the Tambopata-Candamo reserve.

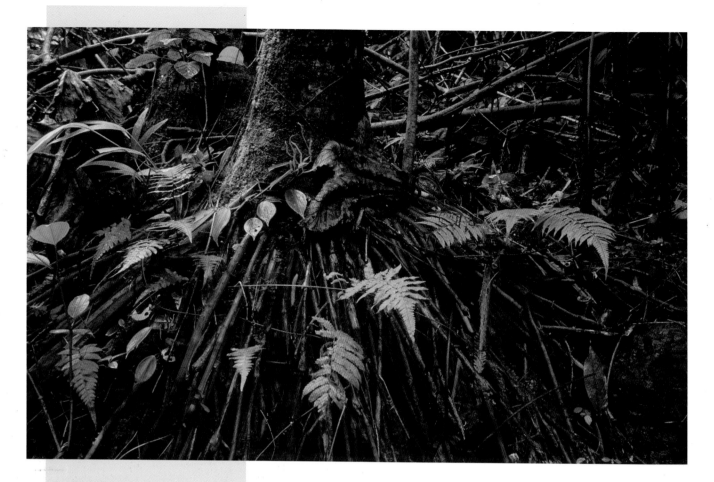

Dense growth

Dense foliage in the Caribbean National Forest of Puerto Rico. This small region of tropical rainforest has been protected since the 1870s and is one of the earliest examples of a reserve.

An amazing habitat

Tropical rainforests produce half the world's living wood. They are also home to about half the world's species of plants and animals – and those are just the ones we know about, as scientists are still finding new species hidden away in the depths of these dense, green environments. Rainforests occupy about seven per cent of the land worldwide, yet they contain 80 per cent of all the green vegetable matter that exists on land. All living, dead and decaying trees and plants are called plant biomass. Scientists have worked out that a rainforest has around 45,000 tonnes of plant biomass in every 2.6 square kilometres, which is more than any other habitat on Earth. Each square metre of rainforest produces about two kilograms of new plant growth every year. Typical farmland, by comparison, produces around 0.7 kilograms. This means that rainforests produce about 66 per cent more green matter than farmland does.

Trees are the foundation of the rainforest. They provide food, shelter and precious nutrients when they die and decompose. Take the trees away, and nothing else – not even the soil in which they grow – will survive.

Temperate rainforests

Temperate rainforests grow in wet, temperate climates in coastal regions around the world. The trees, plants and animals in temperate rainforests are very different from those in tropical rainforests. Although they are smaller overall, temperate rainforests have suffered from human exploitation in much the same way as tropical rainforests.

Temperate rainforests are characterized by huge and often very ancient trees, such as the Douglas fir and Sitka spruce. Temperate rainforests in north-western America have been called Cathedral Forests because of their enormous height – up to 85 metres – and the great sense of space beneath their branches. Long grey-green epiphytes, plants that grow not from the ground but from other plants, hang from trees in these forests, and because the climate is so damp, **mosses** grow on everything. Usually, there are many rotting branches and trees on the ground.

Temperate rainforests are full of long-established plant life called old growth. In Oregon and Washington, it is estimated that between 80 and 90 per cent of the old growth has been cut down in the last few hundred years. This is a great loss, as it takes at least 200 years for this complex habitat to mature. Many creatures have suffered from the loss of temperate rainforests and some have been put on the endangered species list.

Threatened species

The northern spotted owl, a threatened species that lives in the old growth temperate rainforests of America's Pacific North-west. More than 80 per cent of its habitat has been cut down.

A green environment

A tropical rainforest is a green world. The green leaves of the forest's plants and trees interact with the intense sunlight and the plentiful rain to provide the primary source of all energy in this environment. Therefore, the colour green not only defines the rainforest environment; it is the very source of its existence.

The different layers

Tropical rainforests are typically structured in four layers. The lowest layer is the forest floor. The thick foliage above the floor shuts out most sunlight, so not many plants grow here, although fungi flourish in this environment, as do many types of fern, which thrive in shade and moisture. Where large forest trees have fallen and allowed sunlight to penetrate to the forest floor, shrubs and smaller trees take advantage and spring up. The sparse vegetation of the forest floor makes it relatively easy for animals to move around, and this level is home to many of the larger animals of the rainforest, such as gorillas, jaguars, anteaters, wild boars and tapirs. Snakes, such as the anaconda, which can grow up to ten metres long; spiders, such as the red-kneed tarantula and the large bird-eating spider; small mammals; and even some birds have all adapted to life on the forest floor. They need good eyesight and keen senses of smell and hearing to survive here.

The next layer up is called the under canopy. It is made up of small plants and trees, as well as the underside of the leaves of larger plants. It is mostly dark and damp, making it the least inhabited part of the forest. Plants such as ferns and vines growing from and supported by trees do well here, though.

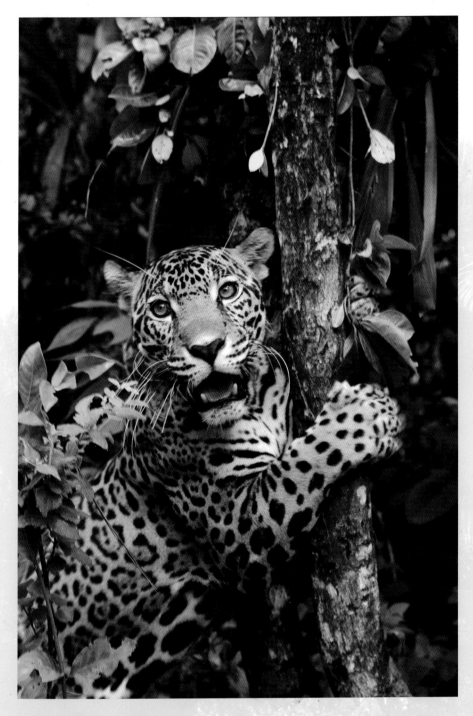

Rainforest cat

The jaguar is the biggest cat in South America, weighing up to 120 kilograms. It lives and hunts in the rainforests.

Human evolution

Scientists have discovered that humans can distinguish between more shades of green than any other colour. They think that the reason for this lies in our evolutionary past. As a species, we evolved over thousands of years in dense forests. It was essential for survival to be able to make out different greens underneath the canopy so that we could spot plants that were good to eat, see the movement of predators and game and find trails.

Insects such as beetles and bees and some snakes and lizards hunt on the tree trunks and branches. Some birds make their nests here, and the occasional big cat, such as the jaguar, will lie in the branches keeping an eye out for prey on the floor below.

The next layer up, the canopy, is between 20 and 40 metres high and is one of the most abundant parts of the forest. It consists of the foliage of trees and forms a roof for the forest. Many animals live in the canopy – including monkeys, orang-utans, sloths, frogs and snakes – and never touch or go near the forest floor. The insects that live in the canopy are the least investigated and catalogued type of animal in the forest.

The highest level, called the emergent layer, is made up of the few very tall trees that have burst out of the canopy and stand on their own – 80 metres or more above the forest floor. These trees have fought their way to the top, and their reward is plenty of sunlight. Animals such as the green-winged macaw and the colobus monkey live high in the emergent trees and never see the lower regions. The harpy eagle, one of the largest eagles in the world, makes its nest high up in this layer but swoops down to feed on animals that live in the canopy.

Hunter at risk

The harpy eagle is an endangered bird of prey and one of the largest eagles in the world, with a wingspan of more than two metres. Its habitat is the threatened rainforest of South America.

Carnivorous plants

*Some plants living in the rainforest have insects on their menu. The soil they grow in is so thin and low in nutrients that they have to supplement their diet. The pitcher plant is one such carnivorous plant. It attracts its prey by its colour and the scent of its sweet nectar, a liquid plant food that most insects find irresistible. However, the edge of the pitcher plant is steep and slippery. When an insect lands to feast on the nectar, it falls into a liquid inside the plant that contains **enzymes**. The enzymes digest the insect and the plant absorbs it as food.*

Gliding around

Animals living high up in the trees of the rainforest have developed different tactics for moving around. Monkeys have four limbs and a **prehensile** tail, which is so useful to them that it is like a fifth limb. Some animals can leap and glide through the air, landing on lower trees. The flying tree snake from South-east Asia does not actually fly, but it too can glide through the air by using its muscles to make its body broader to catch more lift. Other animals that can glide include the flying lizard, which has a flap of skin under its front legs that it uses to glide, and the flying frog, which has flaps of skin on all four feet that catch the air as it leaps out of trees to avoid predators.

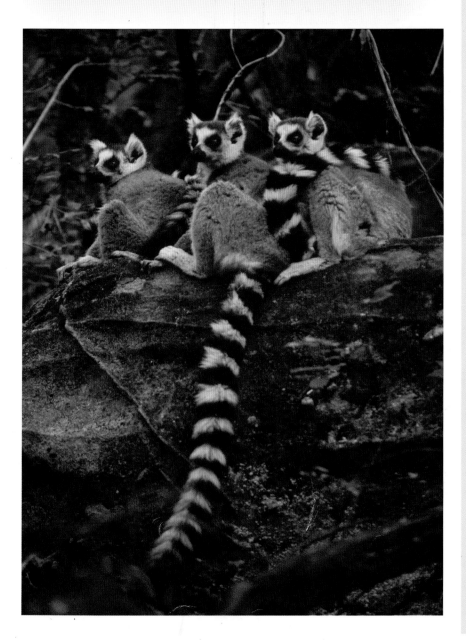

Unique species

Rainforests all over the world are home to animals and plants that have evolved there and are found nowhere else on Earth. These are called endemic species. Often, they have evolved to fill a **niche** in the rainforest. The golden beetle, for example, exists only in the forests of Costa Rica, living on leaves and rotting plants. Islands are particularly rich in endemic species because they are cut off from the mainland. The island of Madagascar, off the coast of Africa, has more endemic species in its rainforests than any other place on Earth. Endemic animals and plants are especially at risk because they live in such a confined region. Once wiped out in a certain area, their gene pool is gone from Earth forever.

Rare lemurs

Ring-tailed lemurs live in the forests of Madagascar. They are on the endangered list of species due to habitat destruction by people living on the island.

Where are the rainforests?

In spite of their huge importance to all life on this planet, tropical rainforests grow only in a narrow band all around the world. This stretches north from the equator as far as the tropic of Cancer and south as far as the tropic of Capricorn. This is because the climatic conditions – constant warmth from the sun and a year-round supply of precipitation – exist only between the tropics. However, there are rainforests on four of the seven continents on Earth: Central and South America, Africa, Asia and Australia.

Central and South America

More than half the world's tropical rainforests are in Central and South America in countries such as Mexico, Brazil, Belize, Guatemala, Costa Rica, Colombia and Ecuador. The mightiest rainforest of all, Brazil's Amazon rainforest, is here. It covers an estimated five million square kilometres and is home to 30 per cent of all known plant and animal species. There are many mammals, such as the jaguar, sloth, tapir, and many types of monkey, including the most agile of all, the spider monkey, and the loudest of all, the howler monkey. Birds are everywhere, creating an enormous variety of colour and noise. Among them are harpy eagles, macaws, toucans, honeycreepers and sun conures. Hunting among the foliage and in the rivers are reptiles such as lizards, caimans and snakes, including the six-metre boa constrictor and the poisonous coral snake. Amphibians, such as the brightly-coloured poison arrow frog, also live here.

Central and South American rainforests are shrinking due to continued exploitation by humans. About 65,000 square kilometres of rainforest are disappearing from this region every year. Logging and clearing trees for farmland on which to grow such crops as rice, sugar cane, soya beans and bananas are two of the main causes.

South-east Asia

South-east Asia has a rich and varied region of tropical rainforests in countries equally diverse – Cambodia, the Philippines, China, Indonesia, Myanmar and Malaysia. The animals of these rainforests include mammals such as tapirs, tarsiers (a type of lemur), orang-utans, gibbons, colobine monkeys, tigers, tree shrews, flying foxes and bamboo rats. There are birds such as hawk eagles, tree swifts, fairy bluebirds, fantails, whistlers, flowerpeckers and wood swallows; insects such as Malayan frog

Huge reptile

The black caiman, the largest member of the alligator family, lives in the rivers and wetlands of the rainforests of central South America. It can grow to be more than four metres in length.

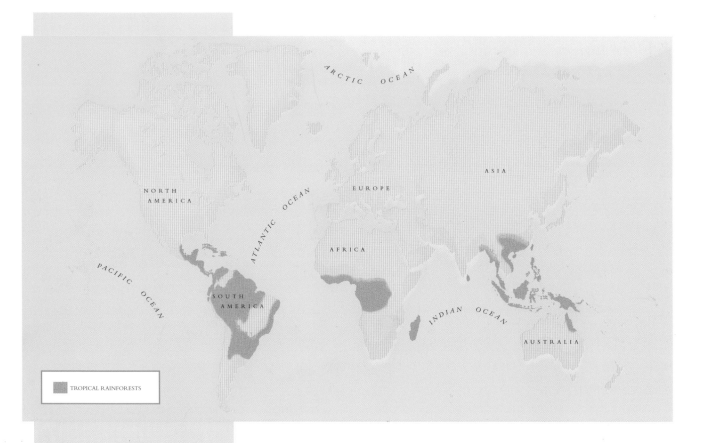

TROPICAL RAINFORESTS

World rainforests

This map shows the main rainforest regions of the world.

beetles, Queen Alexandra's birdwing butterflies, and Goliath birdwing butterflies; and reptiles such as green cat snakes and water dragons.

Like the forests of Central and South America, these rainforests have been reduced in size, mainly because of logging, farming and mining. With so much habitat under threat, many animals have suffered. The orang-utan, for example, once lived throughout the rainforests of China and Malaysia but is now found only on the islands of Sumatra and Borneo.

The island of New Guinea is between 70 and 90 per cent rainforest and includes tropical swamps and **mangroves**. Yet even here the forest is in danger. As the human population has grown, so have the effects of small-scale agriculture. And with logging and mining companies moving in and commercial plantation crops increasing, even this large island paradise is threatened by 21st-century progress.

Africa

There are rainforests in the Congo basin in central Africa and on the coast of western Africa in the countries of Ghana, the Ivory Coast and Senegal. Animals of the African rainforests include mammals such as antelopes, chimpanzees, gorillas, scaly-tailed squirrels, duikers, okapi (a mammal related to, but smaller than, the giraffe), hippopotamuses, black-and-white colobus monkeys, bush babies, pygmy hippos and bats. Birds such as Senegal parrots, Congo peafowl, African grey parrots and scarlet-chested sunbirds also live here.

Africa's coastal forests have been extensively reduced and today exist only in small pockets that are very accessible to loggers and farmers. Rainforests in the Congo basin have fared better, partly because of their greater isolation.

Threatened gorillas

A huge male mountain gorilla. These endangered animals live in the high forests of Rwanda, Zaire and Uganda in central Africa. There are thought to be fewer than 400 left in the wild.

Australia

Australian rainforests are on the coastal fringes in the far north and north-east of the country in Queensland and the Northern Territories. They are home to some of the most unique animals on Earth, found nowhere else. These include mammals such as tree kangaroos, rat kangaroos, opossums, bandicoots and duck-billed platypuses. Birds include cassowaries, brolgas, orange-footed scrubfowls, wompoo fruit doves, topknot pigeons, Australian king parrots, laughing kookaburras and fernwrens. Reptile life includes frilled lizards, carpet pythons, green tree snakes, spotted tree monitors, eastern water dragons and northern leaf-tailed geckos. Insects native to Australia include Ulysses butterflies, zodiac moths, Union Jack butterflies and birdwing butterflies. Amphibians are represented by White's tree frogs, giant tree frogs, striped marsh frogs, northern barred frogs and dainty green tree frogs.

The rainforests of Queensland have been fragmented by logging and road-building companies and by farmers looking for more land for their dairy cattle and crops. Some of the forest is now under government protection.

Australian platypus

A close-up of the duck-billed platypus. This primitive mammal lives in burrows in the banks of rivers in the forests of north-eastern Australia.

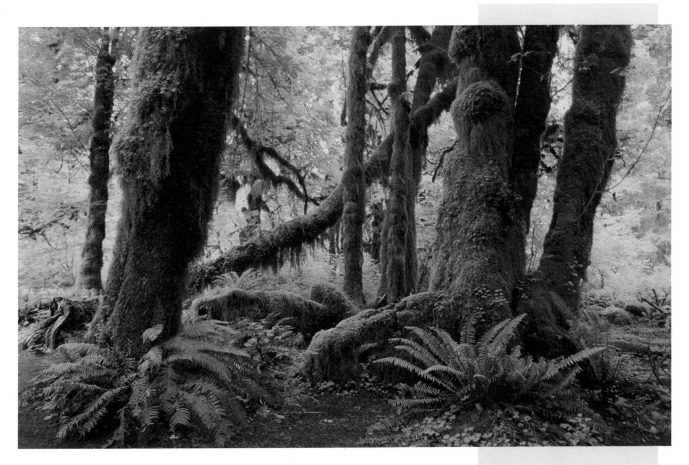

Temperate rainforests

Temperate rainforests need a unique set of environmental circumstances to flourish. These include a high rainfall of two metres or more every year, mild winters and cool summers around 15°C. These conditions exist in only a few places on Earth:

• The north-west coast of North America (Oregon, Washington and Alaska in the United States and British Colombia in Canada)
• The south-western coast of Tasmania, Australia
• Fiordland National Park on South Island, New Zealand
• The south-west coast of Chile
• The coast of Japan
• The south-west coast of Norway
• The Black Sea coast of Turkey and Georgia

The special climate allows the trees in these forests to grow to an immense size. Unfortunately, this has made their wood highly prized by loggers, who have felled the forests in many areas for years.

Moss and ferns

Large ferns and trees covered in moss are typical vegetation in temperate rainforests. This photograph shows the protected Hoh River valley in Olympic National Park in Washington.

Why tropical rainforests are important

Some people wonder why so much fuss is made in the news about the plight of the rainforests. After all, Earth is a huge and dynamic planet in a state of constant change. In its billions of years of history, it has gone from a barren rock to home to millions of types of life-forms. However, take a look at the ten rainforest facts below and consider the implications of the rainforests' disappearance.

1   Rainforests are a major source of timber and are therefore of commercial value.
2   They are a source of medicine and drugs, taken from the bark, roots and leaves of trees and plants.
3   They are a source of food, oils, spices, gums, dyes and natural rubber.
4   The roots of their trees help to bind the precious and fragile soils of the landscape.
5   Rainforests regulate and help to purify the world's water.
6   They enable three-quarters of the world's water to re-enter the atmosphere through **evaporation** and **transpiration** in a vast and complex process known as the **water cycle**.
7   They are a major influence on the world's climate.
8   They play a major role in the **oxygen cycle**.
9   They are the most diverse and rich habitat in the world.
10   They are a main part of the world's life-support system.

Rainforest crop

This farmer is harvesting sugar cane near his village in the northern Philippines. Sugar cane is a rainforest plant.

Economic value

Some rainforest trees are extremely valuable to the modern world. Rubber trees provide people with latex, the milky juice underneath their bark, to make rubber. Hardwoods such as teak and mahogany are highly prized for furniture.

Rainforests are also a great source of food. People have survived in the forests for thousands of years, living off their natural produce. Many rainforest food products are today used all over the world. Some of the most common products include chocolate (from the cocoa plant), sugar cane, sweet potatoes, pineapples, oranges, lemons, bananas, mangos, Brazil nuts, cashews, peanuts, yams, papayas, guavas, avocadoes, coffee and spices such as nutmeg, ginger and cloves.

In addition to providing food and other products, jungle plants have given people some very powerful chemicals and drugs. The rainforest has been called the largest chemist's shop in the world.

Cocoa harvest

This man is harvesting cocoa pods, the raw ingredient of chocolate. The cocoa plant came originally from the rainforests of South America, but today it is grown in Africa, Sri Lanka and South-east Asia.

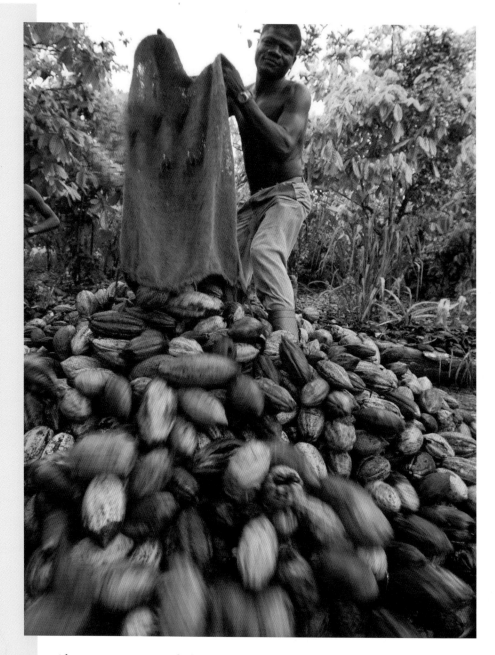

Almost a quarter of all the medicines in the developed world have come from rainforests. Often, the clues about these medicines' benefits were given to scientists by native people who, through trial and error, discovered many healing uses for various plants. The common painkiller aspirin originally came from the bark of a rainforest tree, and quinine – a drug used to help cure **malaria** – came from the red cinchona tree in South America. The rosy periwinkle, from the island of Madagascar, contains chemicals that have helped fight two forms of cancer in humans: Hodgkin's disease and leukaemia. Today, one of the most persuasive arguments for halting the destruction of the rainforests is that such destruction may be causing the extinction of useful plants that scientists know nothing about. In the process, people may be losing life-saving medicines provided free by nature.

Influence on climate and water

Rainforests have an effect on both local and international climate and water supply. On a regional scale, as rainforest trees put water back into the atmosphere they help create clouds, which in turn produce more rain in the region, helping to maintain the rainforest climate. As rainforest trees absorb water through their roots and release it back into the atmosphere, they also filter out impurities in the water.

On a worldwide scale, rainforest trees not only help maintain a healthy balance in the water cycle, they also take carbon dioxide out of the atmosphere through the process of photosynthesis. **Carbon** is stored in the living tissue of the trees, and oxygen is put back into the atmosphere. This process is essential to the health of the planet, since carbon dioxide is the main **greenhouse gas** contributing to the gradual warming up of the world's climate.

The richest habitat

One of the reasons tropical rainforests are so precious is that they are home to more varieties of plant and animal life than just about any other type of habitat on Earth. In fact, the Amazon rainforest is the most species-rich environment on the planet. It contains 80,000 species of trees and 2,000 species of freshwater fish, including the infamous piranha. The area is

Photosynthesis

Photosynthesis is the process by which green plants turn water and sunlight into carbohydrates and oxygen. Only green plants can carry out photosynthesis, because the **chlorophyll** *that makes their leaves look green is a chemical vital to the process. Rainforest plants produce 40 per cent of Earth's oxygen through photosynthesis.*

Food from leaves

A highly magnified photograph of a chloroplast, part of the structure of a leaf that contains chlorophyll. Chloroplasts are vital to food production through photosynthesis in green plants.

Rainforest fish

A photograph of a piranha, clearly showing the row of razor-sharp teeth it is famous for. These fish are native to the freshwater rivers and lakes of tropical central South America.

The area is also home to half the world's known species of butterflies – about 9,000 – including the monarch, malachite, and postman butterflies, as well as more than 3,000 land vertebrate species.

In Queensland, in north-east Australia, the small belt of rainforest covers only one-tenth of a per cent of the total land area. Yet this rainforest contains a high percentage of the overall number of species in the country. It is home to 37 different **marsupial** species, including the tree kangaroo, musky rat kangaroo and spotted-tailed quoll (a small, meat-eating marsupial) and 47 different types of frogs. Sixty-two per cent of the country's butterflies live there, including several huge species, such as the *Aenetus monabilis*, which has an 18-centimetre wingspan, and the Hercules moth, with an even bigger wingspan of 25 centimetres. This part of Australia also has the greatest diversity of bird life in the country. Its 370 known species have such exotic names as the tooth-billed catbird and bridled honeyeater.

Similarly, the rainforests of Costa Rica in Central America are among the most diverse habitats on Earth. Although more than half the overall forest area has been cut down since Europeans arrived in the country in the 16th century, there is still enough rainforest left to sustain about 215 types of mammals, 560 species of birds, 250 kinds of reptiles, and 115 species of fish. Some of these species are on the world's endangered list. Costa Rica has 11 of the bird species on this list, including the harpy eagle, crested eagle and orange-breasted falcon.

Counting species

Counting species of plants and animals is not easy and has long been a subject of hot debate among scientists. More than one and a half million species have been recorded worldwide. However, scientists know that there are many more yet undiscovered. They have estimated that there are between two million and 80 million species of plants and animals altogether on Earth today.

Most of the identified species are mammals and birds. This is because they tend to be quite large and relatively easily seen and classified. Many of the animals and plants remaining to be classified are small, such as insects, worms and fungi. Searching for new species in the depths of a rainforest is difficult, but this is where many of them are found.

Tiny amphibian

A strawberry poison dart frog inside a mushroom in Costa Rica. These tiny animals live in the rainforests of Central America.

Zaire is a country in south-central Africa that has avoided some of the spectacular destruction of the rainforest that many other areas have experienced. About three-quarters of the original tree cover of the landscape in Zaire remains intact today, and the country is like one huge nature reserve, with more types of birds and mammals than any other country in Africa. However, a road-building programme has given people better access to more remote areas, leading to an increase in logging activity in the country.

Rainforests under threat

Rainforests all over the world are under attack. The reasons are simple. Rainforests do not produce much wealth for local people or governments. Felling timber, especially for wood from valuable hardwoods such as mahogany, makes some money. But by far the most profitable thing to do with the land is to clear it for farming. Profits can also be made by mining, extracting oil and even hunting animals to sell as pets or to use their fur.

Our shrinking forests

Rainforests have been shrinking for 100 years or more. They once covered about 14 per cent of Earth's surface. In the worst decade for rainforest destruction, from 1980 to 1990, almost 170,000 square kilometres of rainforest were destroyed every year. To put this in perspective, an area nearly twice the size of Portugal was lost annually. By 1991, half the world's tropical rainforests had been destroyed and in the last decade, about 15 per cent more has been lost for good. At this rate of destruction, there will be no tropical rainforests left by the middle of the 21st century.

Sacred bird

The resplendent quetzal, a bird once sacred to the Mayan civilization of Central America and now the national bird of Guatemala. It is on the endangered species list due to hunting and the loss of its rainforest habitat.

Slash and burn

The life of the great rainforests forms a complex web, both fragile and remarkably resilient. It can cope with certain amounts of change and even damage. For example, humans have lived in these forests for many thousands of years, practising slash and burn agriculture. They make small clearings in the forest by cutting and burning the foliage, and then they settle and grow crops. Usually they move on to another part of the forest after a few years. This allows the forest to recover and regrow. Using this method of agriculture, the level of human interference in the life of the forest remains small and containable for many years.

Today, however, industrial-scale logging and road building into the heart of once-remote areas means that change is happening at a speed and level that the natural environment cannot handle. Even slash and burn agriculture has added to **deforestation** now more people live in the rainforest. With more people doing it, even this primitive practice has become a problem for the forest.

Clearing land

Slash and burn agriculture has been practised for hundreds of years in the rainforests by tribal societies. Today, it is used more aggressively by modern farmers to clear trees and grow crops.

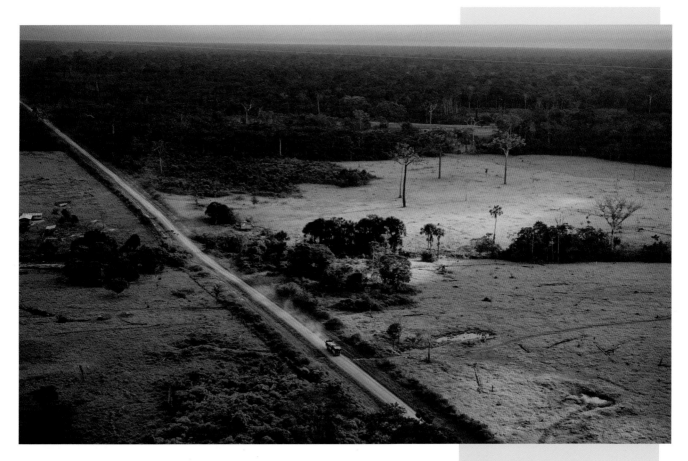

Soil loss

Tropical rainforests are supported mostly by thin soils which are only about 2.5 centimetres deep in places. If there is plenty of tree cover, this is not a problem, as tree roots and other plants help to keep the soil in place. The soil is replenished by the natural cycle of death and decay; branches, leaves, insects, animals and birds all eventually die and fall to the forest floor, where termites and fungi help them to decompose. Because of the jungle's heat and humidity, decomposition and the release of precious nutrients back into the growing cycle occur relatively quickly.

However, when trees are cut down, powerful tropical rains soon sweep away the vulnerable soil, causing infertility. Even if trees are replanted, it takes 50 years or more for the soil to recover. Cutting down large areas of rainforest can also increase the number of floods in a region. This is because trees help hold on to water, both in their roots and within their leaves. Without them, rainwater can pour across the landscape.

The changing rainforest

A changed landscape in Peru – ancient, virgin rainforest and land cleared for farming adjoin each other. A new road provides loggers and farmers with access to even more remote parts of the rainforest.

29

Lost to farming

A section of the Amazon rainforest being felled and burned to provide space for cattle farmers.

Non-sustainable farming

People have cleared huge areas of rainforest to graze cattle. However, this has proved **unsustainable**. Within a decade the land is useless. It loses all its nutrients and farmers have to move elsewhere to graze their cattle, felling more trees to do so, and leaving behind a small desert. Such **desertification** occurs for several reasons. The most important is that the trees have been removed, so the soil is easily washed away. In addition, cattle eat the ground cover and prevent any regrowth, and their hoofs damage the thin soil.

Logging in Indonesia

Indonesia, a country in tropical South-east Asia, is made up of more than 13,000 islands and has a population of more than 200 million people. There are about 300 different ethnic groups, including many tribal peoples from the extensive rainforests that carpet vast areas of these islands. Today, loggers bulldoze dirt roads that penetrate into the heart of remote and previously inaccessible forests, home to native tribes that have lived in isolation for hundreds, if not thousands, of years.

Once roads have carved lines of communication into the dense forests, local hunters and farmers move in to exploit the opportunity they provide. They build small homes that then become permanent. Eventually, small settlements grow in the forests and turn into larger villages, and the remoteness of the area is lost forever. New areas are cleared for further farming, native peoples are driven away, and wildlife comes under increased threat. Erosion follows the clearing of the trees, and, eventually, the land becomes barren. This process is not unique to Indonesia. It is fairly typical of most tropical rainforest regions.

Destruction of the Amazon rainforest

The Amazon rainforest is not only the largest rainforest in the world, it is also one of the most ravaged. As with many other forests, road-building deep into the heart of the landscape has opened the door to further development by farmers, miners and loggers. Much of the most destructive development started in the 1960s and was financed by the **World Bank**. The Trans-Amazonian highway (Belem-Brasilia highway) was built more than 40 years ago and proved to be the first of the huge roads that opened up the heart of the rainforest. It was part of a government programme to move poor, landless people from the more populated south and east portions of Brazil on to land cleared in the rainforests. Deforestation increased a great deal during the 1970s and 1980s as room was made for these new settlers. Native peoples in very small numbers had lived in Rondonia, a region in the far west of the country, for thousands of years. Suddenly, from the 1970s onwards, more than 50,000 people a year arrived to farm the land. This massive change put enormous pressure on the land resources, especially the thin rainforest soils.

Growing soya beans

In a world in which farmers produce food for markets thousands of kilometres away, land use can change very quickly to suit the tastes of consumers. Today, many people in Europe eat soya bean products for their health. The beans are low in fat and cholesterol and make a good substitute for milk and cheese. Many soya bean crops grown in America have been genetically modified, which is not what European consumers want. As a result, farmers living in rainforest regions in South America have started growing non-genetically modified soya beans for European markets. Although they can make a good profit from these crops, they need to clear a lot of rainforest land to grow them. In Paraguay alone, almost one million hectares of rainforest have been cleared in the last ten years for this crop.

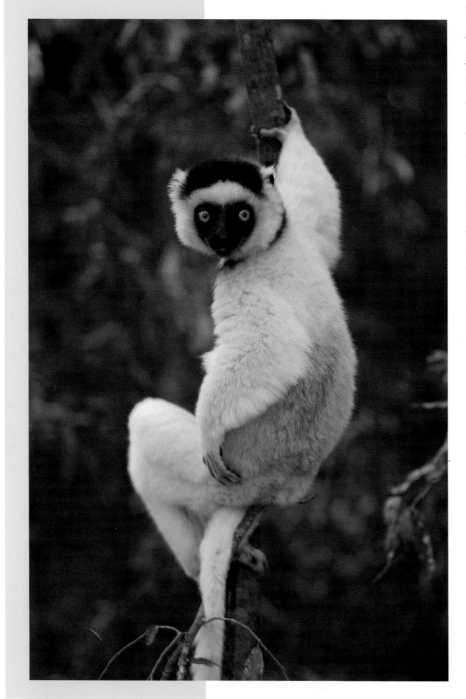

Lemur at risk

Verreaux's sifaka lemur, found in the wild only on the island of Madagascar, is currently on the vulnerable species list.

Endangered animals of the rainforest

The number of endangered species in the rainforests is increasing. This is due to the destruction of their homes and over-hunting. Here is a short list of just some of these animals. And do not forget that plants are endangered as well.

*Aye aye, a small **primate** from the island of Madagascar*

Boa constrictor, from Central and South America

Caiman, a reptile from Central and South America

Congo peacock, from Africa

Golden lion tamarin, a mammal from the forests of Brazil

Gorilla, from the African countries of Zaire, Rwanda and Uganda

Harpy eagle, from Central and South America

Jaguar, from Central and South America

*Kinkajou, a small, **nocturnal** mammal from Central and South America*

Lemur, a small primate from Madagascar

Loris, a primate from South-east Asia

Okapi, a mammal from the forests of central Africa

Orang-utan, from the South-east Asian islands of Borneo and Sumatra

Queen Alexandra's birdwing butterfly, found only in certain forests in Papua New Guinea

Scarlet macaw, from Central and South America

Tapir, a mammal from Asia and Central and South America

Tarsier, a small mammal from the Philippines and Indonesia

Endangered species

The World Conservation Union is an organization formed in 1948 by the United Nations. Its original name was the International Union for the Conservation of Nature and Natural Resources, or IUCN. This organization produces and updates a list of plants and animals around the world that it classifies as endangered. It keeps this information in what is called *The Red Book*. The book lists more than 12,000 individual endangered species, many of which are found in rainforests around the world, and most of which are plants. The endangered species count rose by 2,000 species between the years 2002 and 2003. This rapid increase may be explained in part by scientists being better able to study and record species than they were in the past. However, there can be no doubt that the movement towards extinction is speeding up partly because change brought about by human activity is accelerating all over the world.

Hunted to the brink

The tapir is a secretive mammal related to the rhinoceros. It lives in the jungles of Central and South America and South-east Asia. It has a small trunk, thick and hairy skin, and a short tail. Tapirs grow up to almost a metre tall and live on plants. They do not breed often, so their population remains small. Due to the destruction of their forest home, and because people hunt them for their meat, they are becoming endangered. The Baird's tapir, for example, is now extinct in El Salvador and Mexico, where it once lived near the river edges of the dense forests.

Tapir threatened

A photograph of the elusive and endangered Baird's tapir, taken in Corcovado National Park in Costa Rica. This mammal likes to live in the heart of the rainforest, close to water.

Trees in danger

Plants, including trees, make up the biggest group on the list of endangered species. They are the habitat that provides a home for animals. So when animals suffer from habitat destruction, this means that trees and plants are being chopped down. One example of this is the caoba tree, found in the Ecuadorian lowland forests. It is a relative of the avocado tree and has been felled for its timber. However, it has recently been cut down in large quantities to make way for banana trees and oil palms – crops that are worth far more money than the caoba tree. This conversion of native forest into plantation crops is an increasingly common problem in rainforests worldwide.

Hunted almost to extinction

The skins of illegally hunted big cats are confiscated by customs officers. Tigers once ranged through central and southern Asian rainforests and grasslands but have been hunted to near-extinction.

6

The future for rainforests

Aside from the many scientific reasons to hold on to rainforests, such as their role in regulating the world's climate, purifying and recycling our water and providing a home for millions of animals, there are also moral questions to be faced concerning the destruction of this habitat. For example, do we have the right to destroy such a fragile but fertile environment? Future generations surely have the right to inherit these wonderful places. 'This we know: the Earth does not belong to man; man belongs to the Earth. All things are connected like the blood that unites us all. Man did not weave the web of life; he is merely a strand in it. Whatever he does to the web, he does to himself.' These are the words of Chief Seattle, a Native American, and they remind us that we have an obligation not to degrade Earth beyond repair, but to take only what we need, so that areas such as rainforests can replenish themselves.

At the same time, people who live in or near rainforests have the right to earn a living. These forests grow mostly in relatively poor countries, where every penny counts. Because the governments of these nations are not rich, they cannot always afford to protect rainforests from exploitation from farming, logging and hunting, since some of the money earned

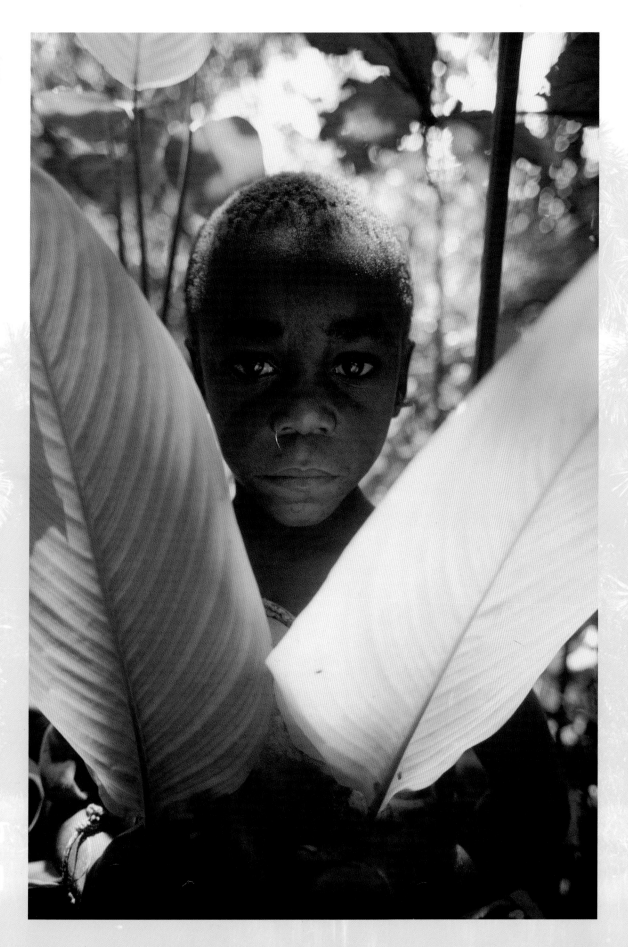

Threatened peoples

A pygmy girl from the rainforests of Zaire (previous page). Her people have lived throughout equatorial countries in Africa for thousands of years.

Balanced lives

Yanomami tribespeople prepare the staple root food, manioc, out of which they make a type of bread. The Yanomami have lived in the rainforests of Brazil and Venezuela for thousands of years without disrupting the ecology of their environment.

Rich and poor

*Most tropical rainforests are in Third World, or developing, countries. These are poor countries in which the people are mainly farmers struggling to survive in a **global economy**. Clearing rainforests to make land on which to grow crops is one way that people can increase their income. It is unfair to expect such people to see the problems in the same way people from rich countries see them. As one farmer said, 'If the West [Europe and America] wants us to grow trees, then they will have to pay us to do so.'*

from these activities is paid directly to the government as a form of tax. Some of these taxes are used to pay for necessities such as clean water, hospitals, schools and public transport. Protecting the remaining rainforests while also allowing local people to live their lives and farm their land is one of the biggest concerns facing the world in the 21st century.

Too little but not too late

Scientists estimate that only ten per cent of the world's rainforests are currently under any form of protection. They believe this is too little to save forests as a habitat with their important **biodiversity**. However, they also believe that there is still time for the people of the world to come together to do something about it and increase the amount of forest protected.

World Bank initiative

The World Bank was set up in 1945, after the Second World War. It is run by the United Nations, and it has lent money to poorer countries to help them develop industry and farming. This has caused problems for rainforests in places such as Brazil, where World Bank money was used to build roads deep into the jungle. However, the World Bank recently joined forces with the World Wide Fund for Nature (WWF) to create a programme called Forest Alliance. This partnership aims to increase the number of rainforests worldwide that are protected from exploitation. Working with governments and private industry to make sure that the forests are properly managed will help to stop the extinction of plants and animals in rainforests. The Forest Alliance plans to create 50 million hectares of new protected forest and to implement effective ways to monitor the areas.

Saving birds

More birds are threatened with extinction in the rainforests of Central and South America and in South-east Asia than in any other part of the world. The latest figures show that there are 113 different species in Brazil and 115 species in Indonesia that are threatened. Today, there are dozens of conservation areas throughout Indonesia and Brazil. For example, Mount Leuser National Park on the island of Sumatra covers 9,500 square kilometres and is one of the largest conservation areas in South-east Asia.

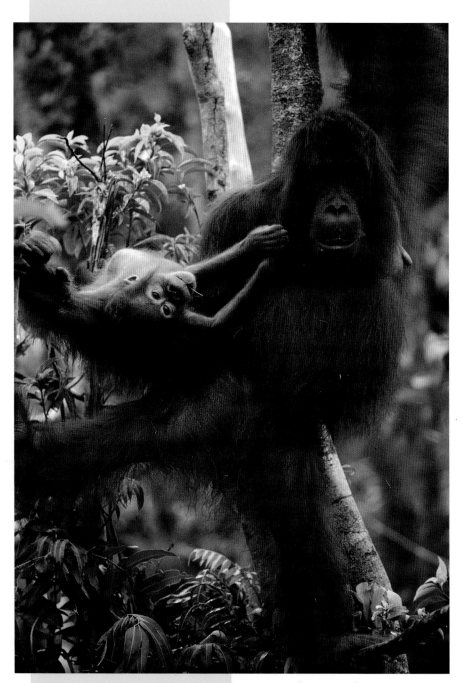

Protected species

This mother and baby orang-utan have been saved from the hunters who have devastated the orang-utan population in Indonesia. They have been released into the Tanjung Puting Biosphere Reserve in Borneo.

Help for the orang-utan

Baby orang-utans have been prized by local forest hunters and **poachers** in Indonesia for many years. This is because people will pay a lot of money to have one as a pet. Before taking the baby away, the hunters first kill the mother, who will otherwise fiercely protect her offspring. This has led to a dramatic decline in the population of orang-utans in the wild. Because of this, the government of Indonesia has now banned people from owning pet orang-utans.

To help animals which have spent time in captivity, rehabilitation centres have been set up. The goal is to educate these primates in the ways of the wild so that they can go back into the jungle on their own. First, the orang-utan is taken to the edge of the forest and allowed to do some exploring, while still fed by its keepers. Then the keepers withhold food for a few days, and the animal has to try to gather its own food from the forest, as its wild relatives would do. The programme has been moderately successful. Many tame orang-utans will never really be able to fend for themselves in the jungle. The best that can be achieved is a semi-wild state in which they are fed and live in protected areas.

Australia leads the way

In 1988, a vast area of rainforest in Queensland was made a
World Heritage Site. It covers almost 9,000 square kilometres
and includes 43 different forest areas and 41 national parks. The
project was opposed at first by the Queensland government
because it gave a high level of protection to the forest, which was
in conflict with the interests of loggers and farmers. However,
tourism is becoming an increasing source of income for the area,
helped by the closeness of the rainforests to beautiful sandy
beaches, a wide ocean and the **Great Barrier Reef**, which is also
a World Heritage Site. The region also contains the only surviving
native Aboriginal Australian rainforest people. They now inhabit
a protected reserve called the Yarrabah Aboriginal Reserve.

It has been estimated that 20 per cent of the original forest cover
in the region is now gone, but that leaves a substantial area of
this precious habitat. It is still logged and farmed, but these
activities are monitored and carried out in a sustainable manner.
In many ways, this is an excellent example for the future. However,
Australia is a relatively rich country. The protection rainforests
receive in this country is likely to be hard to duplicate in poorer,
developing countries.

Forest parks

*A woman walks in the
rainforest in Daintree
National Park in Queensland,
Australia. The park was
created in 1988 to protect
this ancient forest region.*

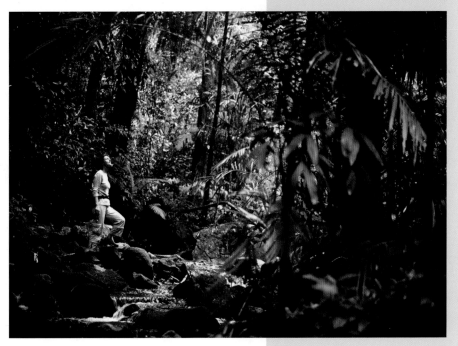

Costa Rica's Amistad Biosphere Reserve

Costa Rican forests have suffered ever since the arrival of Spanish explorers and settlers in the 16th century. More than half the forests are now gone, along with many of the native Guaymi Indians who lived in them. The remaining forests are under threat from copper mining, logging, beef farming, drilling and poaching, as the government of Costa Rica, like so many governments in poor, developing countries, has encouraged farming and mining in forest areas.

In the mountainous region of the Cordillera de Talamanca in the heart of Costa Rica lies a special protected region called the Amistad **Biosphere Reserve**. Due to the protection offered by this reserve, the rainforest destruction has been slowed down, and the native peoples have increased in number, from around 6,000 in 1960 to more than 10,000 today. These are small but significant gains.

Cuban reserve

A small frog sits on a leaf in the Cuchillas del Toa Biosphere Reserve in Cuba. This special place was made a biosphere reserve in 1986.

Tourism in Madagascar

The island of Madagascar, off the south-east coast of Africa, has more endangered primates living in its rainforests than anywhere else on Earth. About 90 per cent of the island's forest and plant cover has been cut down, so the original habitat of these primates has shrunk to a very small proportion. Today, Madagascar, which has more endemic animal species than any other country, is a popular **eco-tourism** destination. So it is in the best interest of the Madagascan government to help save what remains of the rainforests and their biodiversity in order to keep tourists coming to their island.

Eco-tourism, a model for the future

Tourists spend billions of pounds every year on flights, car rental, accommodation, restaurants, entertainment and leisure activities while on holiday. Today, the tourism industry caters to all sorts of different people – from those who want culture and famous cities, to those who want to go deep-sea diving or rock climbing. One of the fastest-growing areas is eco-tourism. People who care about the environment and who want to spend time on holiday among wild animals and plants can choose to travel with companies that aim to minimize the impact they have on the places they visit. Holiday-makers can even opt for a working holiday during which they actively try to improve the landscape by planting trees, cleaning up litter, or monitoring birds, sea creatures and plants.

Places as far apart as Cameroon and Costa Rica have become involved in eco-tourism. They have set up nature reserves, protecting their unique and beautiful wildlife and landscapes. These assets attract tourists, who pay to visit them. The income from tourism pays the wages of the wardens and other workers, helps to maintain the nature reserves and generates tax for the national government. This model could be used by many developing nations which have precious rainforests to preserve. Eco-tourism could become a serious contender to replace logging, destructive farming and rare animal and plant poaching as a much-needed source of income for local communities.

Conservation organizations

The first step in saving the rainforests is watching what we have now and monitoring it in the future. Today, there are many different organizations around the world dedicated to helping and monitoring the rainforest environment. Some are large and involve the help and funding of many countries; others are small and very local. Here are some of the better-known organizations.

• **Friends of the Earth**   www.foe.co.uk
Founded in 1971, Friends of the Earth is now one of the world's best-known and most respected environmental pressure groups.

• **World Wide Fund for Nature (WWF)**   www.panda.org
Founded in 1961, this Swiss-based organization raises money to fund conservation operations around the world, focusing in particular on endangered animals.

• **Greenpeace**   www.greenpeace.org.uk
Founded in 1971 in Canada, Greenpeace has grown to become one of the world's biggest and most influential environmental pressure groups. It campaigns all over the world on behalf of the environment.

• **International Union for the Conservation of Nature (IUCN)**   www.iucn.org
This organization publishes *The Red Book*, which presents the most comprehensive picture we have today of the state of the planet in terms of threats to species.

What you can do to help

Everyone can be involved in helping to save rainforests. Many schools have projects supporting this special habitat. The first step is to become more informed. Here are a few ways you might help the rainforest biome.

• Be careful in selecting plants for your garden or as presents for friends and family. Some rainforest plants are very rare, and taking them from their natural setting to make a profit harms the forest. In some countries, it is illegal to sell rare plants.
• Get involved in efforts to raise people's awareness of the fragility of rainforest environments through projects at school or with local clubs.
• Get involved at school to find out more about the fascinating lives of rainforest animals and the wonderful plants that have evolved to survive in this warm and wet environment.
• Support one of the many environmental organizations dedicated to protecting rainforests. Fund-raising events and awareness days often feature fun activities.

- Have respect for the people who live in rainforest regions.
- Remember, whatever delicate natural environment you find yourself in, take nothing but photographs and leave nothing but footprints. That way, you will always leave wild places in the state in which you found them.

Further reading

Bloomin' Rainforests Anita Ganeri (Scholastic, 2004)

Rainforests Godfrey Hall (Hodder Wayland, 1998)

The Vanishing Rainforest Richard Platt (Frances Lincoln, 2003)

Plants and Planteaters (Secrets of the Rainforest series) Michael Chinery (Cherrytree Books, 2000)

The Living Forests Clive Wilson (Kingfisher Books, 1994)

Ecosystems and Environment Anne Fullick and Chris Oxlade (Heinemann Library, 2000)

Websites

Rainforest Action Network
http://www.ran.org

The Rainforest Site
http://www.therainforestsite.org

Rainforests.net
http://www.rainforests.net

Tropical Rainforest Coalition
http://www.rainforest.org

Tropical Rainforests
http://rainforests.mongabay.com

Oxfam
www.oxfam.org.uk/coolplanet/ontheline/explore/nature/rainforests

Glossary

Biodiversity   The numbers and types of different plants and animals living in a specific environment.

Biosphere reserve   An internationally-recognized conservation area administered by the United Nations Education, Scientific, and Cultural Organization (UNESCO).

Carbon   An element found in several forms and in combination with other elements to form compounds; combined with oxygen, it forms carbon dioxide. All living things have carbon in them.

Chlorophyll   A substance found in most plants that makes them green in colour. It absorbs the energy from sunlight and makes it available to the plant for the production of carbohydrates.

Deforestation   The removal of forests and woodlands, usually by people. Reasons include clearing land for agriculture or industry and timber harvesting.

Desertification   Human actions that turn fertile land into sterile desert, through over-grazing, loss of vegetation and soil erosion.

Eco-tourism   Tourism based upon a more sensitive approach to the impact that travellers have upon the landscapes they visit.

Enzymes   Substances in the bodies of animals and plants that help certain life processes happen. For example, there are enzymes in the digestive system that help to break down food.

Evaporation   When water is heated and turns into vapour, it evaporates. Evaporation is part of the water cycle.

Evolved   Scientists believe that life on Earth has developed, or evolved, over billions of years. The theory of evolution claims that all life has come from single-celled forms and has slowly become more complex.

Global economy   A term used to describe the fact that the economies of individual countries are linked to each other through international trade today.

Great Barrier Reef   The largest group of coral reefs in the world. The Great Barrier Reef stretches for more than 2,000 kilometres off the east coast of Australia.

Greenhouse gas   A gas, such as carbon dioxide or methane, which traps heat in Earth's atmosphere.

Habitats   Parts of an environment which are self-contained, supplying the needs of the organisms that live within them.

Malaria   A disease which is passed to humans through mosquito bites. It causes a very high recurring fever.

Mangroves   Muddy coastal wetlands in which mangrove trees grow.

Marsupial   A type of mammal, defined by a pouch in which it carries its young. Examples are the kangaroo and the wallaby.

Mosses   Plants that do not have any flowers. There are more than 10,000 different species around the world.

Niche   The place within a habitat that each living organism occupies. This includes the way in which an animal or plant uses its habitat – what it eats, where it sleeps and the environmental conditions it favours.

Nocturnal   Something that happens at night. Some animals are described as nocturnal, which means that they come out at night to hunt for food.

Oxygen cycle   The process by which animals breathe in oxygen and exhale carbon dioxide, and then plants convert the carbon dioxide back into oxygen, which they release into the atmosphere.

Poachers   People who illegally shoot animals for meat or to sell to other people as trophies.

Prehensile   Capable of gripping branches.

Primate   The highest order of mammals in the animal kingdom. Primates include monkeys, chimpanzees and lemurs.

Temperate   A term used to describe a climate that is neither too hot nor too cold. Temperate zones are halfway between the hot tropics and the cold poles.

Transpiration   The process by which water is lost through the leaves of plants and trees due to evaporation.

Tundra   Land close to or inside the Arctic Circle, where the layer of soil just below the surface is permanently frozen because temperatures are low all year round.

Unsustainable   Something that cannot be carried out indefinitely.

Water cycle   The natural cycle in which water evaporates from bodies of water and is given out from plants into the atmosphere. Here it eventually condenses again to form clouds and precipitation.

World Bank   A bank set up in 1945 after the Second World War to help restore the economies of devastated countries. It is part of the United Nations.

World Heritage Site   A cultural or natural site that is considered to be of outstanding value to humanity. The World Heritage programme is administered by UNESCO.

Index